The Mindful Business
By: Janessa Jordan-Rowell

"If You Have That Business Mind You Will Succeed"

Introduction Of The Book:

Good and happy to write this book because I have always wanted to write a book on business. I am also in the middle of opening my own shoe store and the name of it is Appleness shoe store owned by me yours truly. So, a mindful business came to my mind because I wanted to write a book for business, but a title did not come to mind until the month of May 2018. Hopefully my readers will read and greatly appreciate my book writing on book title a mindful Business so read up and God bless you. My bright idea of starting a business and becoming an owner is because I started designing shoes online in the year of 2014 for my shoe brand Appleness I design my shoes from a warehouse shoe company named Aliveshoes which is in Italy another country from the United States Of America so I design under them for my shoe brand Appleness and I wanted to turn my brand into my own shoe company under my shoe brand named Appleness. I made that my enterprise name for my company Appleness Shoe Store LLC.

Tables Of Content

Chapter One
Starting A New Business

When Starting a new business this is not easy work because you are starting from scratch as a business owner and CEO you must know what you are doing. I am a new starter to personally speak and from my point of view starting a new business is a good and bright idea for an individual who has already been through the workforce every person in this world has a right to start their own business or own company. Starting a new business is a great and awesome strategy it is good and better to own and have franchises under your name it is a mindful business most people are too lazy and feel that they do not have the time to take out to put their minds to starting a new business I am truthfully happy for all business owners in the world because they had that mindful business mind so first things first start now not later now what are you waiting for? The future is in your hands and whatever comes to your brilliant mind you believe what it tells you so follow your mind if it is telling you to start your own business because your mind is telling you right. I am in my ending ages of twenties and will be pushing thirty years old next year of 2019. I am so thankful that GOD has given me such a smart mind to open up a business this is the best thing that ever happen to me in my life because I really came along way and been through a lot in my life but honestly speaking from my point of view opening and starting a new business is the best decision that anybody in the world could make the creativity of their mindful business speaks for them sometimes I wonder what goes on in other people brains and minds as I can say if you put your mind to it indeed you could do it. When starting your business, you must have the keys and techniques in your mindset this is why I have made this book title a Mindful business I found out that there is a lot of benefits in starting a new business and becoming a business owner it is such a beautiful thing to start out even if it takes you forever to get finish it will get done in true facts. Some people begin to start a new business when they lose their jobs and just would like to branch out on their own to do their own thing and every individual has the right to do that because everybody has an untold story that no one knows about so they identity to their freedom and knowledge they begin to start their own business. An idea is mindful especially when opening a business there are many different varieties of companies under the names of sole proprietorship, C corporation, S corporation, Inc, LLC, partnership, trust, and estate it all depends on what the owner would like to pick for their company for the choice of sole proprietor this is for individuals who are in business for themselves and household employers, partnerships has partnerships and joint ventures, corporations S&C corporations is for personal service corporations, real estate investments trust regulated investments conduits and settlement funds, Inc is for person or people forming it directors and officers purchase shares in the business and have responsibility for the operation, limited liability company is a structure allowed by state statues and is formed by filing articles of organization with the state for an estate is legal entity created as a result of a person's death, and last but not least for all types of trust including conservatorships custodianship, guardian, irrevocable, trust, revocable trust, and receivership. When starting a new business, you must make sure you start preparing and filing documents for your company an also have your corporate kit for your business company and stock certificates. The entrepreneurial venture is to emerge your business into the market place that needs development a viable business model around a product, service, process or platform starting out small is always the beginning process to launching your startup business or company. Some people start their business with a little or no money at all they begin to take out loans to finance their business or they already have money save up for the business to begin and get started all of this takes a lot of energy you must market opportunity and market timing this mindful business, organization or institution. When my mother started her mindful business she went based on what she had taken up in school which was paralegal studies to become an paralegal she now owns her own business and it is a paralegal firm under the name of Tasby's Paralegal Offices Inc she has been in business for ten years the kind of work and business she does is refer clients that has lawsuit cases to lawyers and attorneys that deals with and practice many laws that fits the clients categories of their cases. The more years that your company is in business the more better and reviews you will have as an business owner it is good to be in business for many years and have more than one location once you have settle in the business field also as a business owner you can take your company to different states and countries once you have started a company and business you will automatically get and receive recognition and get recognized in the business magazines, newspapers, internet and other advertising agency for business corporations.

Chapter Two
The Plan

Making big plans for your company and business must be number one on your list make sure you have business cards printed, flyers, post cards, posters, and billboards because this must be a part of your business plan to accustom your company. The bests plan for your business is to have a good also product or merchandise worth selling and know that people will shop and buy. Purchase all your merchandise from manufacturers and name and number all the stock for the business that is exactly what I did for my brand for my business I have calculated up the price number and sizes for men and women and I added up all the size number of stocks to purchase and multiply times it buy the price. I plan to keep a certain number of stock for each of the shoe sizes this is the order from which I have plan to follow for my business. The mindful business plan of your own right by doing the means of tracking your market and adjusting your business plan accordingly create the space for mindful reflection at work foster the skills that are highly critical in the business world to be successful in your business plan unsubstantiated assumption can hurt a business plan the products and services in the mind of your customer knowing what to buy. Plan and have guidance because mindful profits help small business owners will key principles that is planned must be kept the way you have planned it. It is better to plan and build your proposal pay close attention to how much you are bringing in, and how much money you are spending we as human being are actively shaping our minds so why not put our minds to a marvelous business plan with space of freedom and calmness contentment to grow with these mindful plans. As business planners the formal statement is business goals which is attainable and plans for reaching them the plans for a mindful business target intermediate goals business plans are decision making tools and business plans are determined by the mindful goals and audience. A good and great business plan can help to make a good and great business credible, understandable, and attractive to is unfamiliar with the business I am writing a good business plan for my mindful business and it can go a long way towards reducing the odds of failure business plans are made and available to all.

Chapter Three
The Future

The future is in your hands build the reflection of you it is your world that you are creating I have always said that "Creativity Is The Key To An Open Door". That is my quote so create your future of a mindful business influence your mind to think things over about your past, present, and future are you where you would like to be now in your present I have come to a solution that things happen for a reason I sometimes think back on my past and see where I am at in my present and I always said if this situation did not happen to me I would not have Had a business so yes situations do make you and they make you do better feel better and look better it is all shaping your future for you and your life I am thankful that things happen it is all about mindful thinking in some situations some people does not know which way or route to take in life but as I said it is all about mindful thinking always put your mind to the positive on how to overcome these situations so your future will stand and shine within you. All future for business minded people is always bright you know why because they block those negative thoughts and use their useful minds everything you do is mindful when most people see that people are smart and that you have things going for you they try to mess them up this is generally speaking and writing knowledge from the top of my mind and brain negative and nasty people will try to mess up your future and bring you down those type of people are not mindful they are very dumb and if you want a good future you should stay away from those type of people so as I can say the future is yours. No one can ever predict their future we do not know what the future actually holds only God knows, the facts of a future is for you to incorporate mindfulness as a leadership to your own practice it is all about inspiring, guiding, and connecting anyone who wants to explore mindfulness of your future enjoy better health more caring relationships and compassionate future with deep resilience future if a mindful business culture creativity and innovation is the key to a future focus on you and your insights on things well chosen goals and objectives points a new business in your mindful right direction form the road map for your company business future well-being mindfulness is big business mindfulness into the future if you have a mind then you have wealth because what you know can be worth money opinion pieces mindful of the future mindfulness is the essentials to your business. Personal excellence means career, business, studies, money, and wealth leading a new business model for yourself to set your future possibilities of the mind for a better future business owner should always keep in mind with succession because smart business owners Create and plan their succession for the mindful business that they are opening. Success secrets is to value yourself and value your business a vision is a picture or idea you have in mind of yourself your business a clear vision helps you pursue your future dreams and achieve goals an idea of the future the mindful business strong wish a future focused mindset. Future in global environment the business will do extremely well as long as it is global because once your name goes global you are well known worldwide this is the best future insights ethical business minds to build the future and discover your brains magical future in your mindful business what kind of future could blow through your mind finding of the future to business use the knowledge to boost the ranking of your business as long as you have opportunity or was given opportunity you have a future in your mindful business all it takes is peace of mind for your financial future and business the future is based more than just a business book it takes reading to uplift this is the future journey to help a mindful change inside and out individual businesses is an organization which becomes agile as the larger companies themselves. This is the real world completed with real time envision the future as opportunities as well challenges future of business the human endeavor and industrial sector will be immune to the future mindful business yes, the future is coming excellence, technology, brake throughs, new ways, mobilizing talent for business professionals looking to maximize the future if what will be viewed as a standard resource. This is inherently good look and fit for a future for a mindful business what can possibly be the results we do not know the undesirable outcomes on how the business future what will be the annual growth rate of an investment for future business lifestyle shaping the future of humanity business virtual reality mindful business future is emotional intelligence and happiness the prediction is like a forecast. The mindful business future into transforming as you are dwelling on the past anticipate the future which has an impact on you as an entrepreneur.

Chapter Four
Culture Of Creativity

Live the kind of life you would like to live culture of creativity is what make you as a business person and it also gives you strength. I write books and design shoes under my brand and design clothes and it all helps me and strengthen me into the creative butterfly that I am that is my culture of my creativity. Mindful business culture of creativity relates to leading edge thinkers it is personal growth creativity achievement, independence, conformity, control, obsession with opportunity this culture of creativity supports strategic business creativity is overcoming barriers to creativity a creative mind can enhance best ideas to achieve in a business. If you do not culture create for yourself or think for yourself you're not helping yourself culture of creativity is a spiritual and mentally thing to have strong passion within yourself for your mindful business activism, your independence counts and it speaks for you this purpose supports you in your own little way culture of creativity by giving meaning promoting cultural and creative sectors for growth the mindful business in the management of you being more open minded stimulating your thoughts this mindful business that you are creating is your personal discoveries many individuals make culture of creativity so that it is known for them and by them these are the insights of culture of creativity everyday thinking and problem solving helps people face and adapt to charging the world due to their creations a mindful person puts their energy into the mindful business mental energy to culture of creativity spend great time quietly thinking and creating this is what intelligent people does creating stuff that is named after you is a reflection of you pieces creativity launch the workshop of the mindful business creativity is the highest power you have. Culture of creativity is the satisfaction which embody beliefs that enables and encourage creativity it is so important in balancing your culture of creativity it has visible sign and messages. Culture of creativity communicating through symbolic to a mindful business emerging wisdom culture from which you will benefit from a mindful favorable business environment rise like an innopreneur that you are in this culture of creativity this is our belief, values, and traditions.

Chapter Five
Mindfulness

There is mindfulness in everything that you do but be careful in thoughts and feeling the mindful company has strong leaders well versed in mindfulness. When you think mindfulness, it develops you as self-knowledge and leads to what describe you as enlighten to the completeness freedom from suffering this is the reason to why mindfulness is good for a mindful business entrepreneur gain a lot by mindfulness formal meditation the social enterprise being in the state of mindfulness if you have mindfulness you will have a good and great life in the world that we are living in today mindfulness is important especially for a business to run and own your business you must have the right state of mind to do that the mind is the most powerful tube that you have to use to get things straight and in order and if your mind is organized to do that you will automatically have a mindfully business. The techniques to mindfulness is relaxation you are self-curious about whatever arises from your past experiences and opening to accept towards all manifestations to your mindful business creations mindfulness is actually a spiritual center self-discipline mindfulness is good for business and tremendous life benefits because at the ending of the day it all benefits you of your well-being mindfulness is the height of fashion in leadership to development the circles and cycles of business this is workshop of your open space of reality to life from which you need and you will accomplish it is all about paying much more attention to experiments in mindfulness you are aware of what you are doing and what you would like to do you had the choice privileges in all if your decisions that you make this is culture of mindfulness as an entrepreneur building and inventing your work project which becomes a mindfulness environment resilience through your practices grounded in the corporate area approaching to mindfulness organizational performance for business companies mindfulness in business is important to have attention to concentration of principles to what really matters.

Chapter Six
Vision And Clear Sense Of Direction

As I can say my vision has always been 20/20 I have a clear sense of direction to who I am and what I would like to do in the business world as an entrepreneur some people do not know which road they will like to take because at that point in time their thinking caps are not on I remember in school my teachers use to tell me to put my thinking cap on and now today I see exactly why because your mind brain can give you the vision and clear sense of direction as an entrepreneur you are in charge so you are most likely the person to direct your own path and the most high almighty God a leader must always be able to set direction create the sense of shared purpose and guide behavior to their mindful business this requires developing your own clear vision of where you want to go describe this future to others is a simple language and providing meaningful guidance regarding how to move forward the typical sequence of vision and clear sense of direction effective visions are clear challenging the sense is complexity when creating the business map wayfinding the sense of direction scale knowing clear personal vision provides direction this is your clear mission and vision is promoting a sense of direction is crucial for building momentum. For most business entrepreneur the vision and clear sense of direction is what your personal goals and responsibilities are clear and consistent communications from the highest levels of a business organization breathe life into the vision and clear sense of direction to the establishment.

Chapter Seven
Over Coming Challenges
Collaboratively

There are many challenges in a business, but the question is can you overcome them? Yes overcome your biggest obstacles and find out what the problem is what challenges are you facing I found out that small businesses see their biggest challenges in one year market and budget yourself because challenges plus frustrations equals problems which is normal and is a part of life and business as your business grows you will eventually face challenges but you have to overcome them spend more of the time managing and troubleshooting the issues to those challenges to overcome them it is a working procedure to get this done very soon so that you would be above and beyond overcoming what you already know and in the business field you will not be challenged as much because you will already know the game the mindful business overcoming challenges is in effect in your conditions to your business world challenges are always faced throughout everyone lifetime you have to be ready to take them on and overcome them challenges are best lesson learn challenges makes you more better within the outcome for a business. The successful community of your business and development from overcoming challenges in time, turf, and trust the mindful business is building to brainstorm and stretch the project ideas that you have in mind overcome challenges collaboratively to the great obstacles to move past them. If you want to collaborate like teamwork you will end up with a great team for your business but it could not always be a great outcome on that because collaboration is inevitable in business by individual, or team and company growth but to overcome challenges by identifying that collaboration to reshape the way humans are getting things done in a business company by shifting from an individualistic mindset to your mindful business from which will make you overcome challenges interdependencies plays a very big role in survival and success for a business.

Chapter Eight
Examine All Forces

The business forces are steps to examine your business strategy what is your purpose and models of examination to analyze the competitive structure to the mindful business industry buying and selling and trends of sales and profits and capitalize the value of the business and expectancy of a return on Investments this is all forces to analysis clearer understanding entrepreneur goes to improve their chances of global success independent practices that all vying for a piece of the business pie all external forces is affect to the origination and operations of business. The examination for all forces is from top to bottom up and down like the stock market mindfulness is big business bring the business counter terrorism forces in the world of business to life this is steady and powerful to everything in the path targets business market threatening in existence which is internal factors in having a mindful business as a bless body of soldiers.

Chapter Nine
Mindful Company

Discovering the arts in your mindful company is focusing on creating every day and reminders for an inspired mission driven approach to the lifestyle business this is the features a shop to buy thoughtfully designed and made by you encourage individuals to live mindfully through opening a company the brand that advocates the idea of a mindful company a bless spotlight that belongs to you, your goods to sell productive and engaged to the world through decade experience and workforce and always make your employees happy appreciate them and welcome them with open arms and heart this is your general audience promote mindful business homage to hope of kindness I believe that each life is cherished as customers oriented individual to join the sales daily in the mindful company creation to help people become their greatest selves and settle their thoughts in the mindful company these are the resources to achieve specific goals mindful business entities with an aim of gaining a profit mindful companies is the association of a person who can be created at law as a legal person so that the mindful company in itself can accept for the civil responsibility which has offshore jurisdiction in the business world the corporate person hood of a mindful company conference in the business field deliver your massage as a presentation fearlessly and manifest your next big idea engage in the mindful company culture.

Chapter Ten
Investing

Investing under your company name is the best solution for your mindful business it will benefit the future for it service industry is the factories for manufacturing in product development investing is financial assets which include capital gains, income, dividends, interest the historic return comes over a period of time. Investing employs accounting ratios, such as earning per share and sales growth to identify securities trading at prices below their worth for high rising free cash flow investing tend to make a company more attractive to investors alternative investors, traditional investments, capital accumulation, capital gains, tax, diversification, foreign direct investment, fundamental analysis, fundamental analysis software, hedge fund, market sentiment, mortgage investment corporation, socially responsible investing, specialized investment fund , technical analysis, time value of money good mindfulness in investing money good roads to take for decision makers high profitability of segment is capital intensive for a mindful business best basics of portfolio allocation.

Chapter Eleven
Sustainable Growth

There is meeting of the minds to think and have sustainable growth and it is all for a good cause sustainable way of life for everyone innovate and lead the mindful business sustainable corporate social is like a grown for fiber sustainable growth is much needed in a business this is the outcome of having a mindful business it makes you grow and you will have a marvelous life that you created for yourself you have planned to grow into your business and grow from it making you shaping you into the person that you are grown like seeds from the ground which is sustainable growth. Many individuals who has become business owners and branched out on their own they have come a very long way so holding on to their creations of business for years makes them grow and eventually the mindful business expands and sustainable growth to become larger and be well known and recognize for the products of sell growth happens throughout those years of withstanding of your business company things happen to grow you and make you better as a business owner that is why you take the odds and make them even whatever does not grow you get rid of it immediately as soon as possible sustainable growth is the realistic attainable growth that a company could maintain without running into any problems a small business can grow without needing new financing there are many mindful business financial resources. Smart people achieve sustainable growth through their mindset of the business this is the bottom line of the results to sustainable growth be more focus on environmental sustainability on global mindful business capitals of effects to growth a company always have an opportunity to grow self-contradictory as prose owners of a business matters in a future that merges economic growth with social responsibility this is a natural system of sustainable growth to the business awareness growing as a human being needs while preserving the support system to their life delivery of competitively priced goods and services that satisfy human need and being quality of life the sustainable growth is progress and have an impact and resources intensity throughout the life cycle the growth has standards of excellence which enterprise products solutions mindful business strengthen you growing you in your industries to profit from it sustainable growth for the business to proper.

Chapter Twelve
Goal

What is your long-term goal? Making, creating, planning your mindful business is a big goal there are many goals to concur short term goals and long term a business is considered a long-term goal to me this was my biggest goal to accomplish for my future for myself. I have always wanted to design and create artistic item products named after me I am so proud of myself that I have well-chosen this goal for my mindful business keeping things on the right track and to keep things that way for your business you must have goals because that is the key to your success to make you successful in your life you will become in order to achieve your goals which is the real benefit so start your goal settings on your mindful business practice you can make it happen be mindful because it has an impact on your life for your mind to think things over for the goals that you are preparing executing your business goals. The system plan to achieve your goals property set is reached ultimately make or break challenges that would empower and focus on the mindful business around the world put yourself in a better position to succeed this is the personal mission statement for your business individually for your organization with editable mindfulness map being who you are and knowing the important things that you have to do for your mindful business is goal setting mind causes us to fixate on track and how we can become more responsive to the richness and complexity that each moment presents setting goals can help keep you motivated on what needs to be done and help you achieve more in your professional and personal life visualize your mindful business goals keep an open mind and heart about change that you desire promote your business and the kind of work that you do live out your dreams achieve your goals and resolutions keep this constantly in mind the envision belongs to you.

Chapter Thirteen
Achievements

Achievements is the number one priority for a business encouraging higher levels of performance and most powerful for a small business entrepreneur advancement is the result of being attuned to every move and decision made in achievements of your mindful business streamline your working process and progress inspirational achievements by improving the company that you have or owning now in the moment of time carry out all responsibilities for the achievements of business. When people go to build their own empire, they are making a difference in the world individuals who have at mindset is blessed persons with a gold mind our human mind is worth a fortune and as humans we are very fortunate to even have a human brain which is a gift and power creative achievements statements which will analyses if you can implement those achievements in a business for you to be a passionate business leader for your mindful business there is no better satisfaction than a achievements you need to engage in better understanding of what you want to accomplish the mindful way will get you where you want to go or want to be earn your worth form a positive patterns to have a successful life and business. Enable all achievements and let go of unpleasant thoughts from which comes to your mind I consider a business a well done true achievement being mindful in the moment can actually change your brain in a myriad of ways this is clearly something that business leaders need to know visualize new paths to achievements when telling a story about your business it helps you achieve and you will always be up to date and top of mind to the business achievements.

Chapter Fourteen
Leadership

Leaders follow their own path to life by the guidance of mindset a mindful business must have dedication and leadership this is the role that is require every business owner to play present new model of modern leadership journey to life being intentional and self-aware is important for any leader in the business field stay open, calm, optimistic, and energized the Shadows of the leadership style impermanent nature of business. Leaders influence the mindfulness for their careers opening up a business is more longer lasting enhancing the quality of life lead yourself by taking change of your attention combine the strong sense of self purpose with your capacity to make that purpose meanful to others being a mindful owner of your personal company leads and well-adjusted employees this is information well written to running a successful business and having natural gifts and talents. Mindful leadership is so powerful deep calm and focus to have presence of mind to face the reality of any situation this is a mind life project in leadership which is highly respected to branding your company compassion strengthening the personal foundation and balancing out work life a leader should not expect others to do the things that he or she is not willing to do that can gradually cause a deterioration of trust leadership is backgrounds to his or her own.

Chapter Fifthteen
Systems

I met the mindful business solutions when it all balls down it results to payroll there are many payroll software systems out for any small business owner to buy and have for their employees when ringing up product sales the system for this is point of sale cash registers from which small businesses turn to the other system is called a credit card machine from which you can charge your customers credit, debit, or gift card those are the main financial management systems for a business. Business system software intelligence tools programming and core features there is art money success to servicing your mindful business. Technology system only the best business gets the benefit of the clear mind hiring, opening, training, inventory systems and expertise to help make your operation a success like-minded business owner who are proactive and engage and want to surround themselves with like-minded people who will pull them into the more successful version of themselves while having a blast along the way having commercial security system is a great way to be secured also having a bookkeeping and accounting system so that things are in track and in order database applications mindful business system. Making sure that there is also camera system surveillance inside your business to record video footage a designed system to capture critical financial operational sales and marketing these are the system introduced in a mindful business highly critical in the business world will be in ordered to perform your business system programs are the hottest business trends wiring software's gaining knowledge being understanding and embodying acceptance of global business solutions.

Chapter Sixteen
Entrepreneurs

Mindfulness is a powerful tool for the most successful entrepreneurs they want to have a hand in every aspect of their business being mindful helps entrepreneurs see the whole picture in front of them embrace mindfulness in a big way it goes from small business mindset to a scalable business mindset the entrepreneur life is the maestro that holds the baton and sometimes almost magically make all parts of your business sync this is your opportunity and recognition evaluation and ethical decision making for yourself as an entrepreneur. Running your own business involves constantly pushing yourself out to let the world know this is who I am this is my creation of my life entrepreneurs are aspiring change makers to elevate their business and life using mindfulness to get regular sleep and making your own schedule this is enough to succeed and sustain a new business goodness is good for business we all are entrepreneurs in the world and have amazing stories to share help give advice and questions to ask and answers to be given the mindful entrepreneur offers a breakthrough and become mainstream if you are starting your own business you are good at something and good at what you do. Entrepreneurship is capacity and willingness to develop as a self-made entrepreneur you must manage your mindful business venture along with any of its risk to make a profit launching the business as an individual or a team identifies responsibilities for the dynamism of industries and long run economic growth for the mindful business simultaneously creating new products including new business models as an entrepreneur you are being responsible for both the ventures success or failure which expose people to the benefits of entrepreneurship understanding their own strengths and weaknesses the mindful business generation propensities for male and female entrepreneurs possess strong negotiations skills and consensus forming abilities. Entrepreneurial firm survival in the mindful business social environmental world which is global leadership and is more customary the transnational in nature to the organization to operate in or provide services, goods for other cultures entrepreneurship determination and motivation is the passion that enriches your conscious business journey.

Chapter Seventeen
Stress Free Workplace

Everyone will love to work in a stress-free workplace I have worked on jobs that stressed me out badly to the point where I resign from them because I started taking that stress home with me and it becomes a major problem working under stress is not good at all too much stress literally causes the human brain to shut down and freeze temporarily dealing with stress, burnout, and other realities of the modern workplace the techniques are often the first experience people have meditation from which is a competitive advantage in the business world your belief about stress clearly affect how being in a stress free workplace improving communication in the workplace physical environment where everyone prospers and business owners oversee everything it is better to open up a mindful business for yourself because in today's economic climate jobs are very hard to come by and it is very stressful to work on them stress is a reaction to too much pressure but some pressure is good and can act as a positive motivator making sure that your workplace is a stress free workplace and a fantastic place to work express ideas workspace cleanness is what is more importantly needed in a mindful business.

Chapter Eighteen
Design

Establish the design for your mindful business necessary changes and interventions needed within the mindful business designing professional life with personal value in mind corporate identities business processes and even methods or processes of designing understood in the terms of discrete sequence of stages development life cycle design literature predictable and controlled manner design production summary of process and results including constructive criticism and suggestions for future improvements perspective in describing the actions of real designers. Designing may be simple repetition of a known preexisting solution creativity or problem-solving skills from designing the business creative profession careers. Design the life for your mindful business to become a great success mindful designs is an innovative and environmentally focused interior styling business the refresh and redesign homes and businesses with the furnishings and accessories already present and use them in a new and inspiring way hacks to our brains design build company with a focus for responsible development create your own mind maps and organize your thoughts with mindful business impressively easy a good design reflects the culture of the business a space with autonomy and flexibility being design is a human centered design collective and digital consultancy that helps the design solutions for mindful business creating stunning design even if you're not a designer mindful business, mindful leadership design strategy lead teams and empower individuals to be supported and become experts. Business design logo for companies and small businesses all over the world pick a winning design it is the process of how integrating mindfulness techniques will help you become a stronger designer and a more engaged team member there are several guidelines to keep in mind what you will be creating whether you are setting up a shop or looking to reach new customers you are going to need an eye catching and stylish business are you ready for a more meanful hobby that not only is a creative outlet but helps you find more joy in your life mindful design the pro tip to have a successful small business brand own a design the beautiful presentations to keep in mind that combines design, business growing let design thinking drive your business there are many aspects to consider particular message to stand out in design stimulate the mind in sense of business purpose within a systemic framework which is global consumer culture business should always be at the forefront of your mind customize storefront and showcase your business as a garden in a creative mindset it is a diploma in design I love the design and desire to be my own boss as a distinct entity I think about design content all the time the mind blowing creative design advertising ideas oriented from designprenurs for their mindful business in the making from them paying attention to human design and implementation.

Chapter Nineteen
Sustainable Business

This is an impact on the globe a sustainable business is needed for future generations to meet their own needs design products that will take advantage of the current environmental situations and how well a company product perform will renewable resources sustainable business enterprise excellence materialities are produced for corporations and consumption of their goods sustainability trend seriously and are enjoying profits financial benefits for the company natural world betterment. The mindful business can transform the life of an individual it can change a life and it can change the world sustainability matters in order to achieve business a conscience to be adaptive in the quality of life for all citizens to create true awareness in a sustainable business being sustainable is just not just about reducing our environmental footprints as a business owner we believe to facilitate and finance society shift to a sustainable business life sustaining products and services.

Chapter Twenty
Successful

Being successful in the mindful business is the visualizing the ideal of new and growing business is a key step toward success keeping the big vision in mind will steer you in the right direction to becoming successful increase your mindfulness and gain more success as an serial entrepreneur and CEO positivity, mindfulness, spirituality, nutrition, health, fitness, wealth, success, business what helps people to be successful is in our professional lives is not such a great idea in our personal lives competition is a quality that comes to mind your subconscious mind contains a powerful force that can make you successful in your mindful business it helps determine your success in many areas of your life successful business people conducts themselves weather that business is on behalf of small company a globe spanning corporation or your own entrepreneurial venture can be considered a successful business person it is important to know how to make money the mindful business opens the doorway to loving kindness which is at the heart of business success.

The End

www.ingramcontent.com/pod-product-compliance
Lightning Source LLC
Chambersburg PA
CBHW021912170526
45157CB00005B/2052